It is springtime at a pond.

W9-AWQ-220

A jellylike cluster of eggs floats among the waterweeds at the pond's surface. These eggs are the beginning of . . .

FROGS

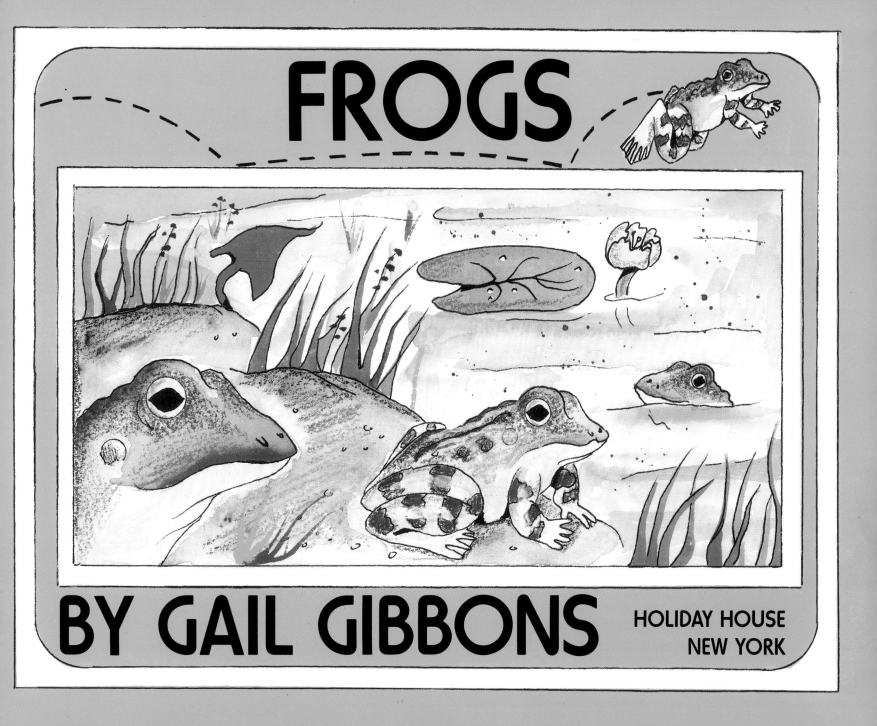

BY GAIL GIBBONS

HOLIDAY HOUSE
NEW YORK

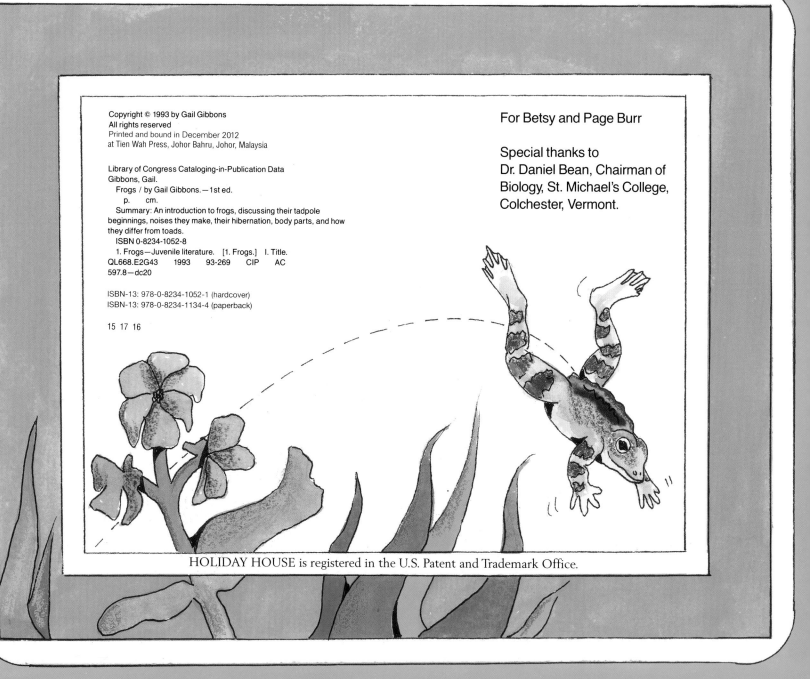

Copyright © 1993 by Gail Gibbons
All rights reserved

Printed and bound in December 2012
at Tien Wah Press, Johor Bahru, Johor, Malaysia

Library of Congress Cataloging-in-Publication Data
Gibbons, Gail.
    Frogs / by Gail Gibbons. —1st ed.
        p.   cm.
    Summary: An introduction to frogs, discussing their tadpole
beginnings, noises they make, their hibernation, body parts, and how
they differ from toads.
    ISBN 0-8234-1052-8
    1. Frogs—Juvenile literature.   [1. Frogs.]   I. Title.
QL668.E2G43   1993   93-269   CIP   AC
597.8—dc20

ISBN-13: 978-0-8234-1052-1 (hardcover)
ISBN-13: 978-0-8234-1134-4 (paperback)

15 17 16

For Betsy and Page Burr

Special thanks to
Dr. Daniel Bean, Chairman of
Biology, St. Michael's College,
Colchester, Vermont.

HOLIDAY HOUSE is registered in the U.S. Patent and Trademark Office.

FROG SPAWN

A breeze ripples the surface. The floating clump of eggs is called frog spawn. Frogs lay their eggs in water or wet places. Otherwise, the eggs could dry up and die.

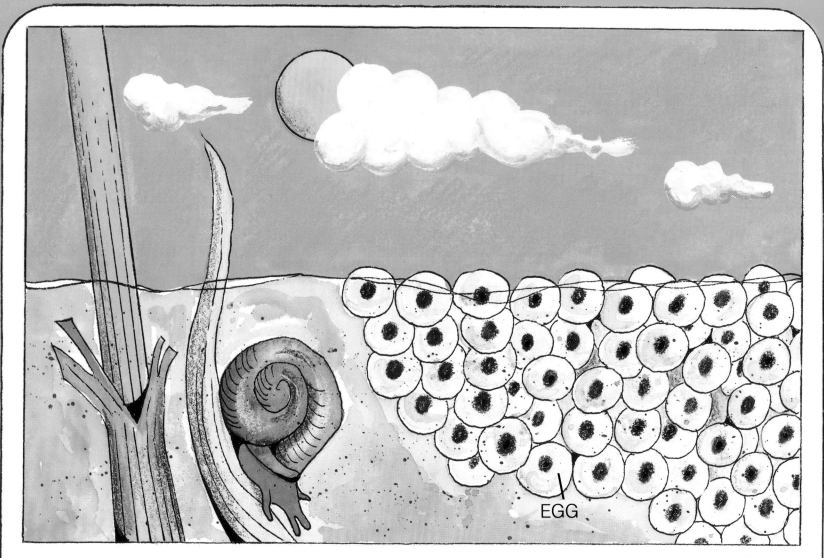

EGG

These eggs do not have shells. They are inside jellylike coverings. As they float, the jelly lets the sun's warmth come through to the eggs inside. Not all the eggs will survive.

Most of the time the large and slimy mass of eggs is too slippery and too big to be eaten. This is nature's way of protecting them. But some of the smaller clusters of eggs will be eaten by creatures living in or near the pond.

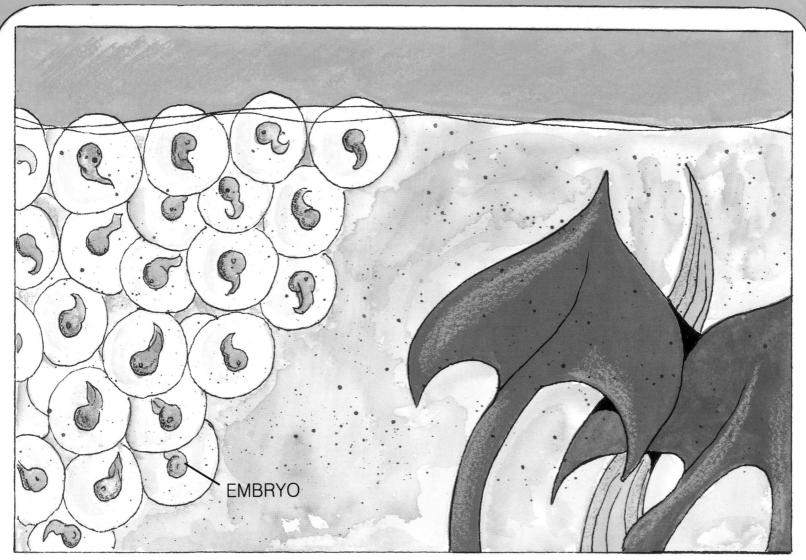

EMBRYO

The dark centers of the eggs slowly grow into frog embryos. The embryos grow until they look like small tadpoles. Tadpoles are frog babies. As they grow, they feed off their own egg yolks.

TADPOLE

The tadpoles grow until they are big enough to break free into the water. It can take from three days to three weeks for this to happen, depending on what kind of frogs they will become.

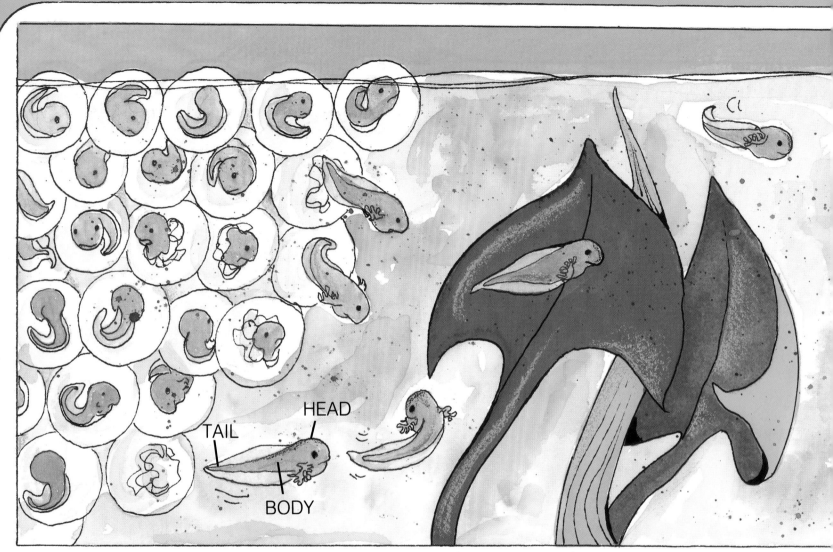

TAIL

HEAD

BODY

One by one the tadpoles hatch from their eggs. They each have a head, tail and body. The tadpoles wiggle their tails to swim.

GILLS

ALGAE

The tadpoles breathe by getting air from the water through feathery outside gills. As they swim, they eat very small plants that stick to larger water plants. These tiny plants are called algae.

One week later the tadpoles look different. They are bigger. Their gills begin to shrink. A flap of skin slowly grows over them. The tadpoles' mouths become hard with tiny teeth in their upper jaws.

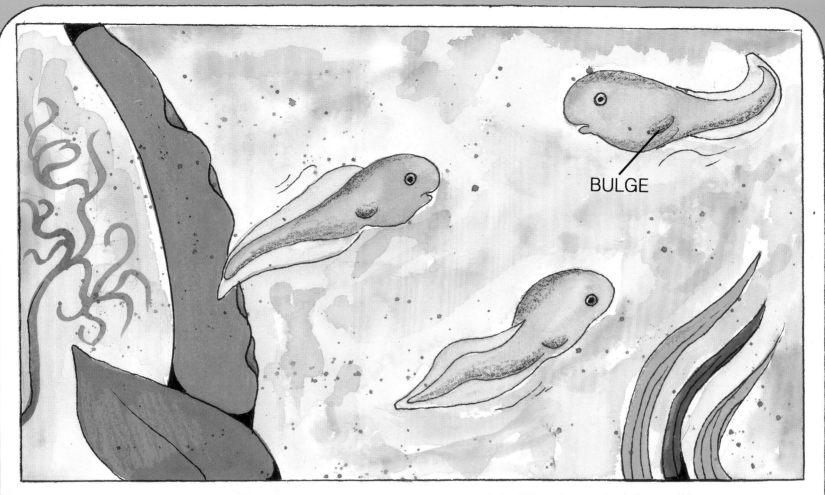

BULGE

Now the tadpoles are one month old. Their outside gills have disappeared. New gills inside the tadpoles take oxygen from the water. Their tails are wider for stronger swimming. Something wonderful begins to happen. At the base of their tails bulges appear. This is where their hind frog legs are growing.

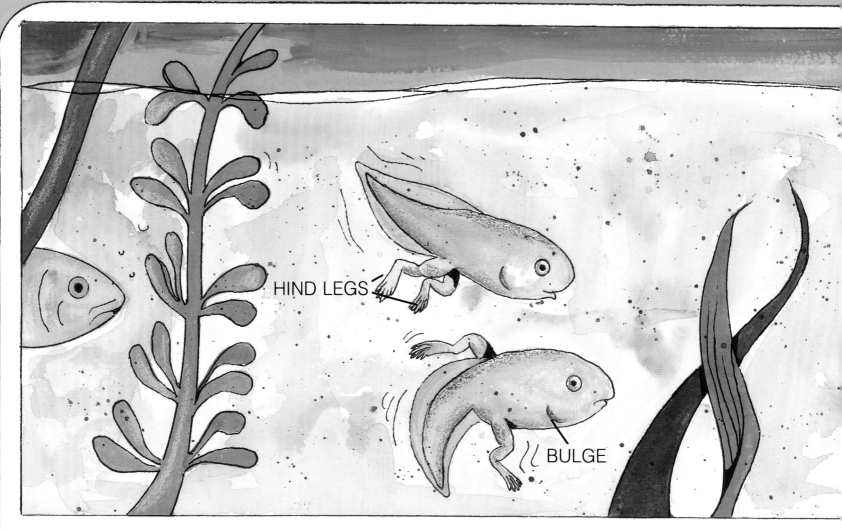

At two months old the tadpoles dart about the pond as they eat. They are still vegetarians. Vegetarians only eat plant life. The tadpoles get bigger. Now they have hind legs. Behind their heads bulges appear where their front legs are growing.

Their tails become smaller. The tadpoles' gills inside their bodies are gone. They have grown lungs to use for breathing. Now and then, they wiggle to the surface to breathe in air.

FRONT LEGS

The tadpoles are about three months old. Again, they look different. They have front legs. Their tails are even smaller. They have shed their tadpole skin and lips. At last, they have the wide mouths of frogs.

FROG

The tadpoles have become tiny frogs. They climb out of the pond and onto the land. Their tails will become smaller and smaller until they finally disappear. The tiny frogs begin to eat insects and worms. They aren't vegetarians anymore.

AMPHIBIAN
(am·FIB·e·an)

Frogs are amphibians. The word amphibian comes from a Greek word that means "two lives." An amphibian can live on land or in the water.

Frogs are cold blooded. That means their inside body temperatures are about the same as the outside temperature. During the next few years, the tiny frogs will grow to be mature frogs. Then they will be able to make their own frog spawn and there will be new baby frogs.

EAR
EYE
NOSTRIL
TEETH
SKIN
BACK LEG
FIVE TOES
FRONT LEG
WEBBED FEET
FOUR TOES
The TONGUE is attached to the front of the mouth. It is sticky.

Frogs have many body parts.

Frogs don't hunt for food. Their big eyes are on top of their heads so they can see all the way around. They stay very still. When something flies or crawls nearby, their long, sticky tongues dart out to catch it. They swallow their food whole.

Frogs that swim use their powerful hind legs and webbed feet to push them through the water. Frogs have two sets of eyelids. One set is transparent so they can see through them. When frogs dive, they close these eyelids to protect their eyes.

On land, the frogs hop about. They use their very strong hind legs to leap. Most frogs can jump ten times their body length. They are wonderful jumpers!

Frogs have enemies. Foxes, snakes, rats, birds and other creatures eat frogs when they can catch them. A sudden leap is a quick escape from danger. For protection, some frogs have skin glands that make them taste bad or make them poisonous. Sometimes their skin color hides them from enemies. This is called camouflage.

CROAK! Frogs make different sounds. Often, male frogs call their mates this way. They pull air into air sacs at their throats. The air sacs expand to look like bubbles. When frogs force the air out of their air sacs and into their lungs, the air passes over their vocal cords which vibrate to make sounds. They make different calls that mean different things. Sometimes frogs are very loud.

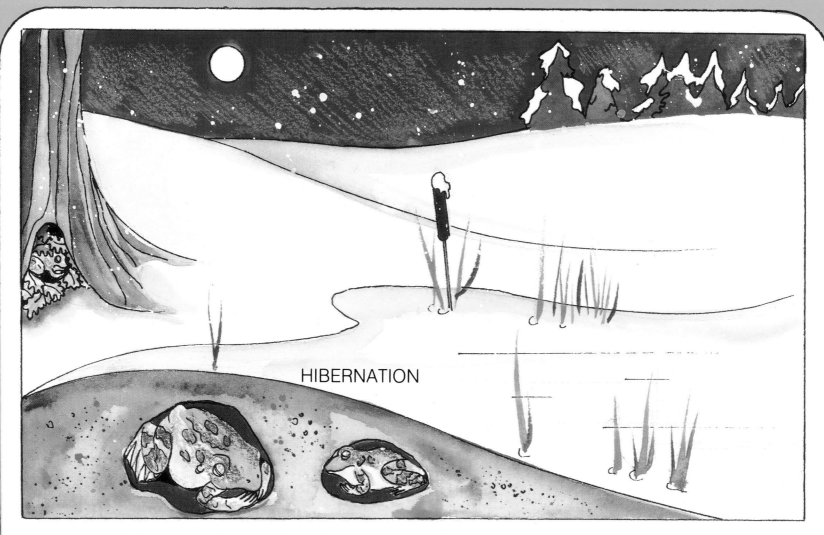

HIBERNATION

Where it is cold in the winter, the frogs go to sleep. Sometimes they find sheltered hollows. Often frogs dig into the muddy bottom of a pond. All winter they sleep covered with mud. They stay completely motionless. This is called hibernation.

In the springtime, when the sun begins to warm up the
ground and the pond's water, the frogs come out of
hibernation. They are healthy and hungry.

People who know a lot about frogs are called herpetologists. They spend lots of time watching and waiting to learn more about these animals. Experts tell us there are more than 3800 different kinds of frogs.

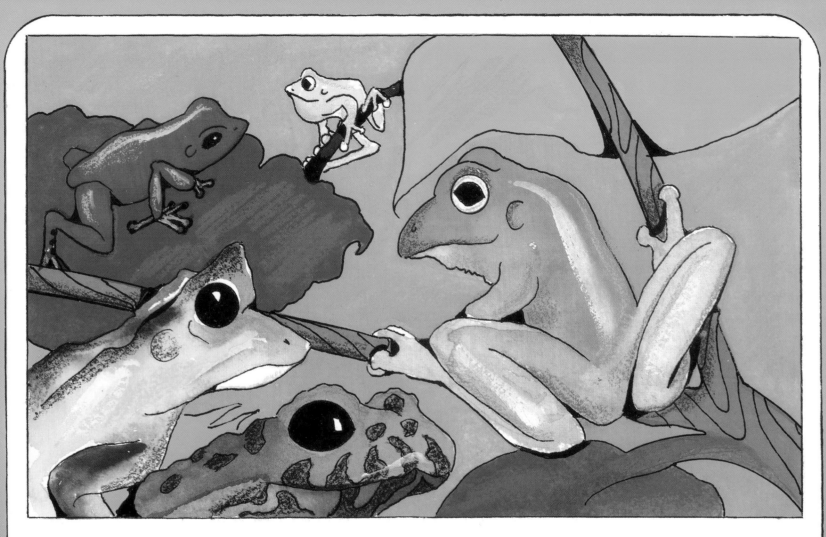

Frogs play an important role in the balance of nature.
They keep insects under control by eating so many of
them. Also, frogs are food for other animals. Frogs are
many different sizes, shapes and colors. It is fun to
learn about them. You can be a frog expert, too!

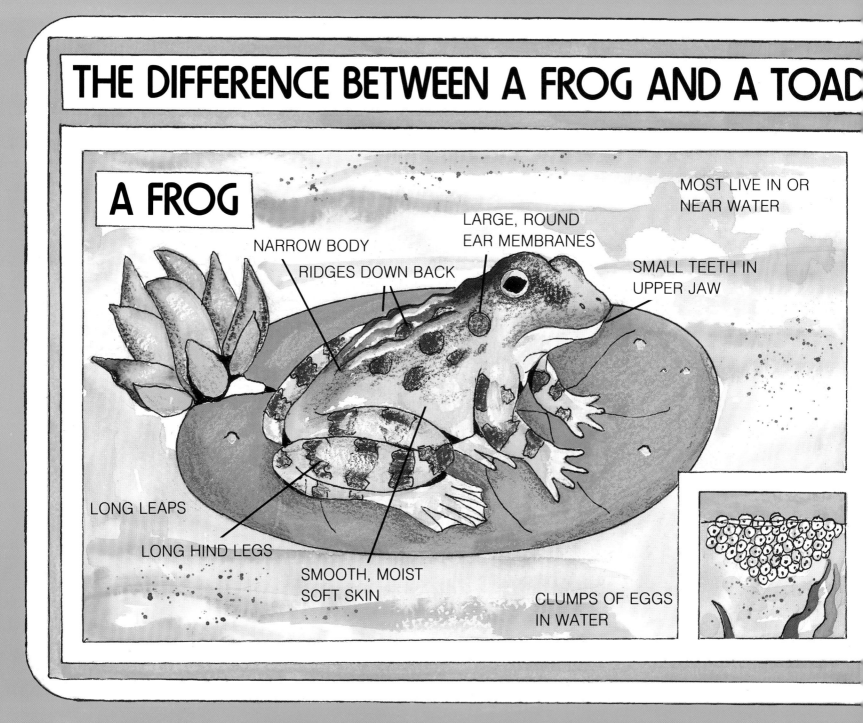

A FROG

MOST LIVE IN OR NEAR WATER

LARGE, ROUND EAR MEMBRANES

NARROW BODY

RIDGES DOWN BACK

SMALL TEETH IN UPPER JAW

LONG LEAPS

LONG HIND LEGS

SMOOTH, MOIST SOFT SKIN

CLUMPS OF EGGS IN WATER

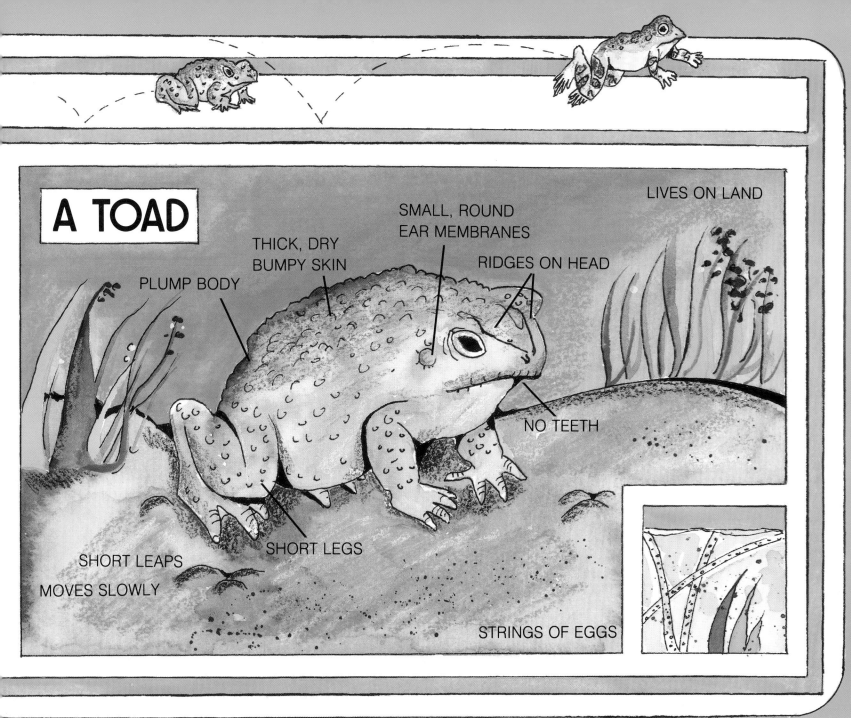

A TOAD

PLUMP BODY

THICK, DRY BUMPY SKIN

SMALL, ROUND EAR MEMBRANES

RIDGES ON HEAD

LIVES ON LAND

NO TEETH

SHORT LEGS

SHORT LEAPS

MOVES SLOWLY

STRINGS OF EGGS

CROAK...CROAK...CROAK..

Frogs lived 230 million years ago, even before dinosaurs lived on Earth.

An African bullfrog can be as big as a football.

Frogs protect gardens by eating huge amounts of insects.

Some people eat frog legs, which they consider a delicacy.

Each year, at the Calaveras County Fair in California, there is a frog jumping contest. Thousands of frogs are entered. In 1860, the famous writer, Mark Twain, wrote a story about this event titled "The Celebrated Frog of Calaveras County."

A dwarf puddle frog can eat 100 mosquitoes in one night.

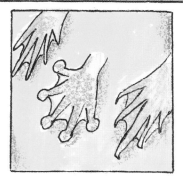

Frogs have different kinds of feet. Some have sticky toes for climbing. Some have pointed toes for digging. Others have webbed feet for swimming.

Some tree frogs spend their entire lives in tree tops and never come down to the ground.

The glass frog has strange skin. You can see through the skin to its insides.

Some very big frogs can eat mice and rats.

Some species of frogs are becoming extinct. Herpetologists are trying to find out what is causing this. We must learn to take better care of life on our planet.